# Political Philosophy

# *Political*
# *Philosophy*

AN INTRODUCTION

## Jason Brennan

CATO INSTITUTE
WASHINGTON, D.C.

**Library of Congress Cataloging-in-Publication Data**

Names: Brennan, Jason, 1979- author.
Title: Political philosophy : an introduction / Jason Brennan.
Description: Washington, D.C. : Cato Institute, 2016. |
    Includes bibliographical references.
Identifiers: LCCN 2016000607 (print) | LCCN
    2016005083 (ebook) | ISBN 9781944424053 (pbk. : alk.
    paper) | ISBN 978-1-944424-06-0 ()
Subjects: LCSH: Political science—Philosophy. | Liberty—
    Philosophy.
Classification: LCC JA66 .B738 2016 (print) | LCC JA66
    (ebook) | DDC 320.01—dc23

Printed in the United States of America.

CATO INSTITUTE
1000 Massachusetts Ave., N.W.
Washington, D.C. 20001
www.cato.org

Libertarianism.org is the Cato Institute's resource for exploring the theory, history, and practice of liberty. Taught by top professors and experts, Libertarianism.org Guides introduce the basic ideas and principles of a free and flourishing society. The core of each guide is a series of short lectures given in a small seminar setting accompanied by a book, very often from the Libertarianism.org *Introduction* series. Guides also serve as a path to further learning. If you'd like to dig deeper, each Guide's homepage offers reading lists, essays, and links to other helpful materials.

Access and watch Libertarianism.org Guides anytime and anywhere, and all for free, at www.libertarianism.org.

# CONTENTS

*Introduction* . . . . . . . . . . . . . . . . . . . .1

1. *Fundamental Values and Why We Disagree* . . .7

2. *The Problem of Justice and the Nature of Rights* 17

3. *The Nature and Value of Liberty* . . . . . . . .33

4. *Property Rights.* . . . . . . . . . . . . . . . .43

5. *Equality and Distributive Justice* . . . . . . .57

6. *Is Social Justice a Mistake?* . . . . . . . . . .71

7. *Civil Rights: Freedom of Speech and Lifestyle* . 89

8. *The Scope of Economic Liberty* . . . . . . . . 101

9. *Government Authority and Legitimacy* . . . . 113

10. *What Counts as "Society"?* . . . . . . . . . 133

11. *Why Political Philosophy Needs*

    *Political Economy* . . . . . . . . . . . . . . 141

*Endnotes* . . . . . . . . . . . . . . . . . . . . 153

*Recommended Readings* . . . . . . . . . . . . 161

*About the Author* . . . . . . . . . . . . . . . 163

*Libertarianism.org* . . . . . . . . . . . . . . . 165

*Cato Institute* . . . . . . . . . . . . . . . . . 167

# *Introduction*

Imagine Virtuous Vani cares deeply about others and is willing to do whatever it takes to save lives. She believes that processed sugar is a scourge killing Americans. So one day she packs a pistol, invades the local 7-11, and declares, "This here gun says you can't sell Big Gulps anymore."

Principled Peter believes that you don't give enough money to charity. You're living high while people die. One day he sends you an email: "FYI:

I hacked into your bank account. I transferred a third of it to poor single moms."

Decent Dani thinks you should buy American rather than German cars. After all, your fellow citizens provide you with roads, schools, and police. You owe them some business. He finds you shopping at a foreign dealer, pulls out a Taser, and says, "You know what? I'll let you buy that BMW, but only if you first pay me $3,000."

You'd probably regard Vani, Peter, and Dani as criminals. How *dare* they treat you like that? You'd want the police to arrest them.

But there's a puzzle here. While the police would indeed arrest Vani, Peter, and Dani, they're also happy to help *other* people—bureaucrats in Washington, Berlin, or Ottawa—do the same things Vani, Peter, and Dani want to do. So this set of examples suggests a few questions: What, if anything, explains why it's wrong for Peter to take a third of your income but not wrong for the government tax office to do so? What, if anything, justifies the Food and Drug Administration in determining what you can and can't eat but forbids Vani from doing so? In general, governments claim the right to do things ordinary people may not do. What, if anything, justifies that?

This is one of the central questions in *political philosophy*. There are many others: What kind of government, if any, ought we have, and what should it be permitted and forbidden to do? Do we have any moral obligation to obey our government's laws and commands? What rights do people have, and why? Should people be allowed to own private property? If they don't have enough property to live well, should the government provide it through tax-funded welfare programs? Should people be free to choose what to eat, how to live, what to worship, what to say, or on what terms they will work? Is it important that everyone have equal opportunity to succeed? Should we make sure everyone ends up equally successful? Should people be allowed to emigrate freely? When, if ever, is war justifiable? What's more important: liberty or equality? And what exactly is liberty, anyway? Political philosophy is the branch of philosophy that attempts to answer these questions in a rigorous way.

In the abstract, political philosophy is the normative analysis of social institutions. Institutions are "the rules of the game in a society or, more formally, are the humanly devised constraints that shape human interaction."[1] For example, if you think about it, democracy and monarchy are really a set of rules about who gets to make the rules. The institution of marriage is a set of rules about how to allocate and control property, children, and sex. The institution of private property is a set of rules about who gets to use, modify, trade, and destroy various goods.

Political philosophy tries to determine the proper standards by which we can judge institutions as good or bad, just or unjust. Of course, to pass judgment on institutions, we usually need to know how they actually work and what the alternatives are. For that, we need the social sciences—economics, political science, sociology, and anthropology. Still, the social sciences alone aren't enough to determine which institutions are best. The social sciences can tell us what the trade-offs are—for instance, that strict economic equality might come at the expense of economic growth—but they don't tell us which alternative to take. Is it better to be equal but worse off, or is it better to be unequal but better off? To answer that question, we have to think critically about justice. We'll have to know how to weigh equality against freedom or prosperity.

This is a primer on political philosophy. My goal here is to give you a working knowledge of many of the major issues, ideas, and arguments in political philosophy. I won't be neutral regarding all the theories and arguments we consider, but I'm also not going to try to convince you of any particular ideology.

# 1

# *Fundamental Values and Why We Disagree*

Consider how we evaluate hammers. We think hammers serve a purpose: to pound in nails. We judge hammers good or bad by how well they serve that purpose.

In contrast, consider how we tend to evaluate paintings. Here, we think paintings are good or

7

bad because of what the paintings symbolize, or how beautiful they are, or who made them.

Now consider how we tend to evaluate people. People can be more or less useful or beautiful, and we do tend to care about who "made" them. (After all, most people value their own children more than they do others'.) But we also tend to regard people as ends in themselves—valuable for their own sake.

Now ask yourself, which of these models is the best way to think about the value of institutions? Some people might believe institutions are valuable because of how functional they are, because of what goals they help us achieve. (If so, which goals are we supposed to achieve?) Others might hold that institutions are (at least partly) valuable because of what they symbolize or who made them. (Consider: many people believe that laws, regardless of their content, become

8

just, fair, or legitimate simply if they are passed by a democratic legislature.) Others hold that some institutions are ends in themselves. (Consider: many people believe that democracy is inherently just and that it itself is the ultimate value, even if other political systems perform better.)

People do not merely debate which institutions are just or good: they also debate standards by which we should evaluate institutions. People disagree about what justice requires.

When we see persistent disagreement about justice, we feel tempted to throw up our hands and conclude that there's no truth of the matter, that opinions about justice are purely subjective. But that's a mistaken inference. The mere fact that people disagree tells us little about whether there's an underlying truth. Disagreement is ubiquitous. People disagree about all sorts of things—whether evolution happened, whether vaccines work and whether they cause autism, or whether the Earth is older than 6,000 years—about which we have overwhelming evidence for one side. Political psychologists—people who study how minds process political information—routinely find that most of us think about politics in biased—that is, irrational—ways. [2] It's not surprising they disagree about what the evidence implies.

We don't simply disagree with each other. Most of us also disagree with ourselves.

Most people endorse a wide range of moral judgments. Some judgments are general and abstract (e.g., "All things equal, increased happiness is good"), some are particular (e.g., "What you did was wrong!"), and others are in between (e.g., "Slavery is wrong"). We arrive at these beliefs for a host of reasons. Some we are more or less born predisposed to accept, others we learn at our mother's knee, others we absorb from our peers, and some are conclusions from conscious deliberation.

We have thousands of moral beliefs of varying degrees of generality or particularity. We cannot hold all our moral beliefs in conscious thought all at the same time—we might instead be able to consciously think about only five or six ideas at once. We thus cannot check all at once to ensure that our beliefs are consistent—that is, that these beliefs don't contradict each other. For that reason, most of us endorse a range of moral judgments that conflict with each other and cannot all be true at the same time. Part of what political philosophy does is bring these conflicting beliefs to light and then attempt to resolve the contradiction. Usually, that means giving up some beliefs—the ones we're less confident in—for the sake of others.

For instance, the typical American believes slavery is wrong because people have an inalienable right to be free. The typical American also believes that people should be allowed to do what they want, provided they don't hurt others. Now consider this: Is *voluntary slavery* permissible? Typical Americans have a set of moral beliefs that seem to commit them to answer both yes and no. Or typical Americans believe that people have the right to choose to associate with whomever they want. But they also believe that business owners have no right to refuse service to black or gay people.

Sometimes, when we disagree about political matters, it's because we have different values, but sometimes it's because we disagree about the facts. So, for instance, the left-liberal philosopher Joseph Heath and I disagree about the extent to which government should regulate the market. Our disagreement doesn't result from disputes over fundamental values. Instead, Heath and I have different views about how well markets and governments work or how often markets and governments make mistakes. We have more or less the same standards—we agree about what it means to "work" and to "mess up"— but we disagree empirically about how well markets and governments meet those standards.

For all these reasons, there is no straightforward one-to-one logical correspondence between any set of background moral, religious, and social-scientific views and any particular political philosophy. [3] A left-liberal can be religious or atheistic. A socialist could endorse any of the major moral theories, have no coherent moral theory, or even be a resolute moral skeptic. A libertarian could endorse Austrian economics or accept more mainstream neoclassical economics.

That said, different political philosophies do tend to emphasize one set of principles over others:[4]

• *Classical liberal* and *libertarian* political philosophies emphasize individual freedom and autonomy. They hold that to respect people as ends in themselves, all people must be imbued with a wide sphere of personal autonomy in which they are free to decide for themselves. Most also believe that imbuing each person with this wide sphere systematically produces greater prosperity, cultural progress, tolerance, and virtue.

• *Communitarian* and *conservative* political philosophies tend to emphasize order and community. For conservatives, civilization is a hard-won victory. They worry that the social order upon which we depend is unstable. Maintaining that order requires that people have a sense of the sacred and that they subscribe to common ideals, moral views, or cultural myths.

Communitarians additionally hold that the collective or the group is in some way of deeper fundamental importance than the individual.

• *Left-liberal* and *socialist* philosophies tend to emphasize material equality and equality of social status. They regard equality as inherently fair and believe departures from material equality must be justified. Socialists tend to believe that few such departures can be justified and that private property is a threat to equality. Left-liberals are more sanguine about markets and private property. They tend to hold that inequality is justified so long as it benefits everyone, especially the least advantaged members of society. They advocate having market-based economies but believe that government should rein in the excesses of the market and ensure that each person gets a fair shot at a decent life.

# 2

# *The Problem of Justice and the Nature of Rights*

Twentieth-century left-liberal political philosopher John Rawls characterized a society as a "cooperative venture for mutual gain." [5] In all but the worst of societies, we're each far better off living together than apart. For that reason, we each have a stake in society and in the basic institutions that hold it together and that structure the terms of cooperation.

But while we each have a stake in the rules, the rules can also be a source of conflict. Different institutions—different rules of the game—tend to "distribute" the benefits and burdens of living together differently. Rawls doesn't mean to overstate this. The rules of the game don't straightforwardly translate into particular life outcomes for any of us. After all, how our lives go depends in part on individual choice. Still, the rules make a difference. So, for example, a society with the institutions of medieval Europe or Japan will tend to best reward those born into the right families and secondarily reward those with a talent for fighting. The United States's current institutions tend to most reward those with high IQs or those good at cultivating political networks. The present world order—a world divided into nation-states that forbid most international emigration—tends to favor skilled professionals over unskilled workers.[6]

Most of us prefer having more stuff rather than less. We prefer having higher rather than lower status. So, Rawls said, self-interested people are likely to disagree on just which institutions and rules are best. They each tend to favor whatever rules benefit them. Principles of justice, Rawls said, are supposed to resolve this disagreement in a fair or reasonable way. Principles of justice are meant to determine the morally reasonable way to assign rights and duties and to determine the proper distribution of benefits and burdens of social cooperation.

Consider one simple theory of justice: utilitarianism. In its crudest form, utilitarianism holds we should just do whatever maximizes net aggregate happiness. Pretty much everyone agrees that happiness is intrinsically good and that pain is intrinsically bad. It seems plausible that we should try to maximize the total happiness of society and minimize the total pain. Utilitarianism leaves us with a simple imperative: pick the action that produces the maximal expected net utility. Many economists thus find utilitarianism attractive. It reduces questions of justice to the search for what economists call Kaldor-Hicks efficiency.[7] Many times, when economists or others say they are "pragmatists" who eschew what they regard as hifalutin' theories of justice, what they mean is that they're utilitarians of some sort.

This crude sort of utilitarianism appears plausible at first glance. But it has serious defects. It seems unproblematic for me to make trade-offs with my own welfare. Suppose I cause myself some suffering now to get greater overall happiness later. I could suffer through accounting class to land a better job or accept painful shots to prevent disease. But suppose instead that we make you suffer so I can enjoy greater happiness. Imagine we hurt you to help me. On its face, that doesn't seem right.

Yet crude utilitarianism happily condones hurting you to help me, provided I benefit more than you suffer. That's the essential problem with utilitarianism. It imagines us each to be receptacles for pleasure and pain. So long as we maximize net aggregate happiness, it doesn't really matter whether some people suffer greatly so that others may be happy.

Fiction writer Ursula K. Le Guin's short story "The Ones Who Walk Away from Omelas" illustrates this problem. The story describes an idyllic, almost utopian society. There is no war or disease. Everyone is healthy, beautiful, and happy. However, we soon learn that Omelas has a secret. A single child is kept imprisoned in a closet, filthy, starved, tortured, and afraid. It turns out that, through some sort of magic, torturing the child is what makes the city so splendid. At some point in their education, all citizens of Omelas are brought to see the child. Le Guin ends her story by describing how each night, a few citizens walk away from Omelas.

Omelas appears to be a counterexample to utilitarianism. If utilitarianism were true, then Omelas would be a just city. However, Omelas is unjust. Therefore, utilitarianism can't be true.

In *Anarchy, State, and Utopia*, the 20th-century libertarian philosopher Robert Nozick introduced a similar thought experiment. He asked us to imagine a "utility monster," a person who enjoys watching others suffer more than those others hate suffering. [8] So suppose I am a sadistic utility monster with an almost-infinite capacity for pleasure. Whenever I watch someone being tortured, if that person feels, say, $X$ units of pain, I experience $X^2$ units of pleasure. Utilitarianism implies that if a utility monster existed, we "should all be sacrificed in the creature's maw, in order to increase total utility."[9] Utilitarianism implies we are morally obligated to feed ourselves to the utility monster. That seems absurd.

Some people might complain that these thought experiments are unrealistic and therefore tell us little about what's right and wrong. It's not clear what force such objections have. In fact, we have little trouble making moral evaluations of unrealistic circumstances. The Force in *Star Wars* isn't real, but even my young children can judge it's immoral to use the Dark Side of the Force. Godzilla isn't real, but if you produced a moral theory that implied "you should feed your kids to Godzilla for fun," the theory would be, for that very reason, absurd. The purpose of these thought experiments is to isolate the various morally relevant factors, and they are designed to be extreme in order to make the problems clear and vivid.

If you find that unsatisfying, note that we have less extreme versions of such problems in the real world. Governments frequently make decisions by which they might exploit or harm the few to help the many. Consider, for instance, the United States deciding to bomb a city block to kill a terrorist, knowing it might kill 50 innocent civilians for every terrorist. Or suppose the French government ponders imposing a wealth tax, harming the few to help the many.

Nozick and Rawls both concluded that utilitarianism fails to respect the "separateness of persons." The idea here is that all people are ends in themselves with separate lives to lead. They are not tools to be exploited for maximizing aggregate utility. We cannot force people to suffer for the sake of others. Thus, they both argue, to respect the separateness of persons, we might see them each as having an extensive set of *rights*. The child in Omelas has a right not to be tortured even if that would maximize utility. Rights are trump cards that forbid people from using us to further their goals.

Early 20th-century legal theorist Wesley Hohfeld argued that one person having a right entails corresponding duties on the part of others. For instance, if I say, "I have a right to life," this means, "Other people have an enforceable duty, owed to me, not to kill me." When I say, "I have a right to free speech," what I mean is, "Other people have a duty, owed to me, not to interfere with my speaking or punish me for it." When I say, "My sons have a right to parental care," what I mean is, "My wife and I have a duty, owed to them, to feed and care for them." In short, to say a person has rights is to say other people have enforceable duties toward that person. [10]

Note that to say you have a right to do something does not entail that it's right for you to do it. It means others shouldn't stop you from doing it. For instance, I have a right to advocate Nazism. I shouldn't—it's an evil view—but I should be allowed to do so.

In *Anarchy, State, and Utopia*, Nozick argued that a theory of justice could give rights a central place but still fail to think about rights the right way. Imagine a "utilitarianism of rights." This theory would hold that we ought do whatever minimizes rights violations. This utilitarianism of rights would still fail to take rights seriously. This theory would still sanction frequent serious rights violations, provided doing so leads to fewer net rights violations. Many of the familiar counterexamples to utilitarianism remain. For instance, Omelas violates the child's rights, but in doing so minimizes net rights violations. After all, it has no crime other than the torture, and so it has fewer rights violations than Denmark or Sweden. Or to take a real case, the U.S. government spies on us, but it claims to do so to stop others from violating our rights even more. So, Nozick might say, the U.S. government cares about rights but not in the right way.

Nozick argued instead that rights are *side constraints.* They tell us what we *can't* do. Sure, all things equal, we should choose institutions and actions that tend to minimize rights violations, but we should do so without first violating others' rights. The *nonviolation of rights* trumps the protection of rights. To give an example, suppose (I think contrary to fact) that allowing the Federal Bureau of Investigation (FBI) to engage in warrantless wiretapping tends to minimize total rights violations. A side-constraint view of rights would hold that this is wrong: the FBI cannot violate rights in order to minimize the violations of these rights.

To hold that people have rights or to conclude that utilitarianism is false is not to say that consequences don't matter. On the contrary, as we'll see below, one of the most common arguments on behalf of rights is that respecting rights as side constraints itself tends to produce good consequences. Though it might sound paradoxical, the argument is that forbidding individuals (and government) from violating rights, and setting constraints on their pursuit of utility, itself tends to maximize utility. That is, forbidding people from trying to do whatever it takes to maximize their own prosperity can itself help to maximize everyone's prosperity.

So far, we've just been analyzing how rights work and why they're important. But this leaves open many questions:

1. Which rights do we have?

2. How strong are these rights? Are they absolute or merely *pro tanto*?

3. Can we alienate or forfeit some of these rights?

To say a right is absolute is to say it's always wrong to violate it and no other consideration can outweigh it. To say a right is *pro tanto* is to say there is a strong moral presumption against violating that right but that sometimes, in special circumstances, other moral considerations can outweigh the duty to respect that right. Many philosophers, including Nozick and Rawls, think rights are probably not absolute. We cannot violate people's rights for just any reason or just to gain significant amounts of utility. So, for instance, if outlawing Mormonism in the United States somehow led to a 20 percent boost in gross domestic product over the next 10 years,

29

that would not be a sufficient reason to violate rights. However, perhaps the duty to respect rights can be outweighed by a concern to "avoid disaster." So suppose the only way to stop the spread of a horrific disease is to quarantine everyone who is currently in a hospital where the disease was detected. Perhaps this would be justified.

To say a right is *alienable* is to say it can be transferred to others—that is, that one person can lose the right and another person can acquire it. Some rights—such as rights to a guitar—are alienable. You can sell or give away a guitar. Other rights might not be. Suppose I, Jason Brennan, wish to sell myself into slavery, provided the slaver pays my family $100 million. Most people think I don't have the right to sell my rights.

To say a right is *forfeitable* is to say that if people act in certain ways they can lose that right. For instance, if I leave my bicycle in the woods for 20 years, never touching it, I might lose my ownership rights over it. It reverts back to the commons. Anyone who finds it can claim it. Or suppose I walk into a public park and start shooting at some kids. In that case, people would be free to kill me to stop me from shooting, and so I would at least temporarily forfeit my right to life.

It's a platitude that one person's rights end where another person's begin. My right to free speech doesn't mean I have a right to show up in your house at two o'clock in the morning to recite Slayer lyrics. Your right to own a baseball bat doesn't imply a right to smash up your neighbor's Corvette.

Thus, the thing a theory of rights must do is clear up what the boundaries of our rights are. For instance, it's obvious that my exerting a weak gravitational pull on your house as I walk by doesn't count as trespassing, but throwing a party there without your permission does. But there are some harder cases. For example, how about letting your dog defecate on my lawn so long as you immediately pick it up?

# 3

# *The Nature and Value of Liberty*

The United States touts itself as the "land of the free." Before we can assess whether it deserves that label or whether that's a label worth having, we need to know what freedom is.

The early 20th-century political philosopher Isaiah Berlin, in his famous essay "Two Concepts of Liberty," claimed that historians have documented over a hundred different ways natural English speakers tend to use the terms "liberty" and "freedom."[11] In natural language, the terms do not have one meaning. That said, Berlin identified two principal ways philosophers and others have tended to use the terms, which he dubs negative and positive liberty.

Negative liberty connotes the *absence* of something: impediments, constraints, interference, or domination from others. So for instance, the American Constitution is supposed to protect freedom of speech by prohibiting Congress from passing laws interfering with one's exercise of speech. Or when we talk about "free trade," we mean an economic system in which no one stops you from trading with foreigners. In both cases, freedom connotes the *absence of interference* from others.

Positive liberty connotes the *presence* of something, usually some power, ability, or capacity. Berlin meant "positive liberty" to refer to the capacity of self-mastery—that is, the ability to choose one's goals and actions in a rational, autonomous way. [12] However, in contemporary philosophical writing, it's more common for "positive liberty" to refer to the *capacity to achieve one's ends or goals.* So, for example, when we say a bird is free to fly in a way I am not, we don't normally mean to suggest no one is stopping the bird from flying. Rather, we mean the bird has the *power* to fly while I do not.

Positive liberty so defined is tightly connected with wealth. As the contemporary Marxist political philosopher Gerald Cohen once argued, "To have money is to have freedom." [13] He claimed that money, or more precisely, the real wealth that money represents, is like a ticket that gives people access to the world. The more wealth one has, the more one is able to do, and in that sense, the more freedom one has.

Berlin, and many other political philosophers in his wake, believed these different conceptions of liberty naturally led to different political ideals. As a result, debates about the meaning of liberty were often seen as *ideological* battles. Many classical liberals and libertarians claimed that if "positive liberty" really were a form of liberty, then this would naturally tend to license socialism and an expansive state, which would use its power to force us to be free. Many Marxists and socialists enthusiastically agreed. They claimed that so-called "negative liberty" is close to worthless without legal guarantees that people would enjoy positive liberty. They claimed that a socialist society would guarantee that everyone had sufficient wealth to lead a decent life, and for that reason, socialism would be superior to market-based economies.

These old and tired debates on the meaning of the terms "freedom" and "liberty" probably rested on a series of mistakes. The problem was that both classical liberals and socialists more or less assumed that liberty was by definition a thing that ought to be protected, promoted, or guaranteed by government action. If you make that assumption, then of course the question of how to define our terms becomes an ideological battle.

But there's no reason to *assume* that. On the contrary, the proper philosophical method would be to first clarify the meanings of the terms. Once one settles on an account of what liberty is, one can then ask what kind of value, if any, that kind of liberty has. The point of defining "liberty" is not to settle debates about its value but to enhance them by making it clear what is being discussed.

There are at least two basic kinds of value any given form of liberty might have. Liberty could be intrinsically valuable, instrumentally valuable, or both.

To say liberty is intrinsically valuable means it is valuable for its own sake or as an end in itself. For instance, one might think it is good if people do not wrongfully interfere with each other, even if noninterference does not lead to any further positive result. Many liberals and libertarians say that to respect others as members of the moral community and as ends in themselves, we owe them an extensive sphere of personal liberty. I should respect your right of free speech even if there's no utility to be gained from doing so.

You don't need some grand moral theory to think we owe each other liberty as a matter of respect. In commonsense moral thinking, we presume that we may not interfere with, attack, or steal from one another. I'm not allowed to swat a cigarette from your mouth or force you to read fine literature, even if it's for your own good. We may not kidnap people and force them to fight our enemies. We may not walk into their businesses and tell them how to run things. We may not force them to serve a good cause or stop them from worshipping the wrong god. Libertarians (and to a lesser extent, left-liberals and American conservatives) think these commonsense moral principles apply to some extent to government as well, while communitarians and others disagree.

To say liberty is instrumentally valuable is to hold that protecting or promoting liberty tends to lead to other valuable consequences or outcomes. For instance, 19th-century economist and philosopher John Stuart Mill argued that freedom of conscience, thought, and lifestyle produce scientific and social progress. [14] (We'll look at his argument in more depth below.) Economists standardly hold that protecting economic freedoms makes people wealthier.

Settling what *kind* of value liberty has does not settle *how much* value it has. In particular, a person who thinks liberty only has intrinsic value does not necessarily hold it has more value than the person who thinks liberty has instrumental value. The first person might think liberty is an end in itself but not a very important end, while the second person might hold that liberty, though valuable only as a means to achieving other goods, is extremely important. (Similarly, oxygen is not an end in itself, but few things are more valuable to us.)

Suppose socialists are right: having the power to achieve your goals is an important kind of freedom, and wealth tends to help people acquire this kind of freedom. Suppose we also agree that as a matter of justice, it's important that this kind of freedom be widespread, that everyone enjoy it. One can accept all this and still favor capitalism over socialism. In fact, this could be one principled reason why we should favor capitalism over socialism. After all, it's an *empirical, social-scientific* question which economic system (or mix of the two) best promotes and protects freedom so defined. In fact, standard textbook economics holds that free trade, private property, and a market economy are important because they tend to promote positive freedom, while socialism is bad because it tends to undermine positive freedom. Some socialists claim positive liberty is an ideal, but that doesn't imply socialism delivers much positive liberty.

It is possible for a laissez-faire capitalist and a socialist to have exactly the same values and to share a conception of freedom and of its value. In this case, their dispute is not moral or philosophical. Rather, it is over a set of empirical claims about how the world works and what it takes to achieve those values in the real world.

**4**

# *Property Rights*

A property right is not one right. Rather, it's more like a *bundle* of rights. For example, to say that country-music star Brad Paisley owns a Fender Telecaster guitar means the following:

1.  Paisley may use the guitar at will. That is, under normal circumstances, he can feel free to use it when he pleases, how he pleases, provided he respects others' rights.

2.  Paisley may alter or even destroy the guitar.

3. Paisley may sell, give away, rent, or otherwise transfer the guitar to others.

4. Paisley may use the guitar to earn income.

5. Paisley may exclude others from using, changing, destroying, or interacting with the guitar. Others may not use the guitar without his permission.

6. If others harm or destroy the guitar, they owe him compensation.

7. Other people have an enforceable moral duty to respect 1–6; they are morally obligated not to interfere with Paisley as he uses, modifies, transfers, excludes usage of, or destroys the guitar. [15]

Together, these rights give Paisley a wide degree of control and discretion over an object and at the same time prevent other people from exerting control over that object.

As ownership is a bundle of rights, we can own different things in different ways. Sometimes we own things, but this ownership doesn't include all the particular rights listed above. For instance, Paisley also owns a dog, Holler. But the way Paisley owns Holler isn't the way he owns a guitar. He can smash a guitar on stage if he wants to, but he can't smash Holler on stage, even though he owns him. So it goes with other things we might own. I own a tennis and pool club membership that I'm allowed to rent out, but it comes with a restrictive covenant that restricts the amount I can rent it out for. My uncle owns a house, but it comes with a restrictive covenant forbidding him from painting it bright pink.

Now that we've settled on what property rights are, we can ask a wide range of normative questions: Should people be permitted to have private property? Should governments or collectives be allowed to own property? What can and cannot be owned? (For instance, may people own a factory or a store?) How strong are these rights?

Eighteenth-century philosopher Jean-Jacques Rousseau famously complained that inventing the institution of private property was a mistake:

> The first person who, having enclosed a plot of ground, thought of saying *this is mine* and found people simple enough to believe him was the true founder of civil society. What crimes, wars, murders, what miseries and horrors, would the human race have been spared by someone who, pulling up the stakes or filling in the ditch, had cried out to his fellow humans: "Beware of listening to this imposter. You are lost if you forget that the fruits are everyone's and the earth is no one's!" [16]

In Rousseau's eyes, humanity might have been better off without property. Following my suggestion above that we might think of institutions as being like hammers, Rousseau might have said the purpose of the institution of private property is for some people to smash others over the head.

Rousseau had a point. Property rights, including *collective* or *governmental* property rights, have to be justified. We need to ask, if property rights didn't exist, would it be necessary to invent them?

Imagine a sparsely populated world in which no one yet owns anything. In this world, all people are at liberty to go anywhere they please, eat any fruit they come across, and sleep anywhere they want. But now suppose a person encloses a plot of land and claims it as his own. It seems that in the first instance the putative landowner reduces and limits everyone else's freedom. They used to be free to go anywhere,

47

but now this presumptuous jerk claims they can't go *here*. Why should anyone play along?

The 18th-century philosopher John Locke famously answered this question by arguing that people who labor in a sufficiently productive way on land (for instance, by farming it) could come to acquire it as their own, provided they leave "enough and as good" for others. [17] But one might object that this standard—leave enough and as good for others—is impossible to satisfy. After all, hardly any new land is being created. If I enclose two acres of land, that leaves two acres fewer for everyone else. If I snatch a gallon of oil out of the ground, that leaves one gallon less for everyone else.

The contemporary philosopher and economist David Schmidtz has a two-part response to this worry. First, he notes, the objection seems to get the facts backward. The objection asks us to imagine early settlers dividing up all the unowned land among themselves. When we latecomers arrive, all the land is taken, and we latecomers get stuck with nothing. That's not right, though. On the contrary, we latecomers are vastly better off than the original settlers. The average American living today enjoys a standard of living about 60 times (yes, 60) higher than the average European colonist of 1600. [18] Even an American earning poverty-line wages still enjoys a standard of living at least 10 times higher than that of the average European colonist of 1600. [19] (Note that this figure is an understatement: it doesn't include any welfare payments or transfers.) And an American living at what the U.S. government considers the poverty line today has, before welfare payments are included, a standard of living at least 4 times higher than that of the average American in 1900. [20]

We owe this all to markets and economic growth. The wealth we enjoy today did not exist 50 years ago, let alone 2,000 years ago. Worldwide per capita income is at least 15 times higher today than it was 2,000 years ago.[21] Wealth has been made, not merely moved around.

To illustrate: Imagine that in 1000 CE, everything the entire world produced that year had been distributed equally among all living people. In that case, the average standard of living today would be worse than that of Haiti or Malawi. In actuality, the average person living in the world today is about 10 times better off than that.

This economic growth occurred in part *because* people privatized land. Unowned land is typically unproductive land. As Locke himself put it, enclosing and farming a plot of land can render it 10,000 times more productive than leaving it alone in the commons. Under the right market conditions, people will tend to trade the surplus with one another, and everyone will be better off. So, Locke argued (and economists concur), the systematic effect of privatizing unowned resources is to improve everyone's welfare. Privatizing not only leaves enough and as good for others, it leaves more and better for others.

As Schmidtz puts it, Rousseau made a mistake. Rousseau realized that appropriating unowned resources for oneself decreases the stock of unowned resources that can be appropriated, but contrary to Rousseau, it does not decrease the stock of what can be owned.[22] To be sure, privatization limits people's freedom of movement, just as Rousseau complained. But it more than compensates them because the systematic effect of privatization is to greatly increase people's positive freedom to achieve their ends.

Second, Schmidtz argues, not only does the imperative to leave enough and as good for others *allow* us to privatize unowned resources, but it might *require* us to do so. Resources that are left unowned often suffer from what 20th-century ecologist Garrett Hardin dubbed the tragedy of the commons.[23] Hardin worried that when no one owns a resource, people have little incentive to maintain it. Worse, they have an incentive to extract as much value as they can before others do. Even if they want to use a resource over the long term, they cannot because they have no way of guaranteeing others will use the resource sustainably.

To illustrate, suppose 10 shepherds each have a flock of 10 sheep that graze on a common plot of land. The carrying capacity of the land is 100 sheep. At carrying capacity, the sheep are fully fed and are each worth $100 on the market. Each shepherd has

10 sheep worth $100 each, and thus each shepherd's flock is worth $1,000. This means the total economic output of the land is $10,000. But suppose a shepherd decides to experiment with adding an 11th sheep to his flock. This brings the total number of sheep to 101. Because the carrying capacity has been exceeded, the pasture begins to die. Some of the grass does not grow back but turns to dust. There is not quite enough grass to feed the sheep fully. Thus, their wool is not quite as thick and lustrous and their shanks are not quite as meaty. So suppose each individual sheep is now worth only $95. However, the shepherd who added the extra sheep profits. His flock of 11 underfed sheep is now worth $1,045. But adding an 11th sheep does not affect only his own flock. The total output of the pasture is now only $9,595 (101 sheep worth $95 each). Consider what happens to the other shepherds. Their 10-sheep

flocks are now worth only $950 instead of $1,000 (10 sheep worth $95 each). To recover from their losses, they will most likely respond by adding additional sheep themselves. But each additional sheep repeats this pattern—it helps the shepherd who added it but hurts the others. Thus begins a mad scramble to overgraze before the pasture turns to dust.

It's worth pausing here to think about what it takes to justify various rules in the abstract. Consider the game of baseball. The point of the game is ultimately for the participants and audience to have fun. The rules of the game have systematic utility. But the umpires on the field are not supposed to judge individual moves or plays on the field with the goal of maximizing fun. If they did that, it would mess up the game: the game would not end up being much fun. Part of what produces the fun is the tension and challenge created by having set rules. The rules can be changed or modified for various reasons (e.g., to make the game more fun, safer, or faster), but individual umpires are not supposed to change the rules on the field, and individual plays are not supposed to be refereed with the goal of maximizing fun.

Similarly, the Lockean imperative to "leave enough and as good for others" is itself most plausible when seen as part of a systematic justification of private property. It's not plausible if it's meant to govern every individual transaction. It doesn't seem plausible that I should be allowed to homestead some land in Montana only if everyone else benefits from my homesteading. That's probably an impossibly strict standard. Rather, I'm justified in appropriating the land, provided I play by the proper appropriation rules in the game "private property," and the game of "private property" is itself justified in part because it systematically leads to certain results.

In this section, I've focused on the systematic consequences of private property rights regimes. But we should note that there are of course many kinds of arguments for and against property rights (or against certain systems of property rights), some of which we'll discuss below.

# 5

# *Equality and Distributive Justice*

Some people have more than others. Some are born with silver spoons in their mouths. Some hardly have a chance in life. John Rawls, like many other left-liberals, socialists, and others, wondered whether this is fair.

Rawls—a tenured, chaired professor at Harvard—was one of the richest people in the United States during his lifetime and one of the richest people to have ever lived. But as Rawls would say, there's an important sense in which this was *good luck*. After all, Rawls was born with certain intellectual gifts, such as a genetic disposition for high intelligence, creativity, and conscientiousness. He was born into a rich family that nurtured his intellectual gifts, pushed him to excel, and could afford to pay for him to attend a private preparatory school and Princeton. Had Rawls been born with worse genes, to parents with little human capital, or to poor parents, he most likely would not have succeeded. But, Rawls would say, it's not as though he did anything to deserve this good fortune. It's not as if before we are born, our souls take merit tests in preembodiment heaven, and the top-scoring souls get to be born to rich parents while the low scorers get stuck in ghettoes. Instead, Rawls would say, he won the genetic and social lottery.

For these kinds of reasons, Rawls became highly skeptical that any people really deserve their station in life. Even if they succeed because of their good choices, Rawls thought, their background or genes would in some way explain their good choices, and so their success is not deserved. Rawls believed you could deserve some good or bad outcome on the basis of some trait or action (such as conscientiousness, talent, or the decision to work hard) only if you in turn deserved that trait or action. But, he thought, every choice you make ultimately results from your genes or your circumstances, neither of which you deserve. Rawls thus concluded that inequalities in life outcomes couldn't be justified on the basis of desert or merit. Though Rawls thought unequal desert wasn't enough to justify inequality, he did believe inequality was justifiable, provided it makes everyone better off.

Rawls might say, suppose we simultaneously come across some resource that none of us have any prior claim to, such as a pie.[24] The most natural way to divide the pie, the way that would elicit the fewest complaints, would be to give everyone an equal share. However, suppose it's a magic pie. Suppose the pie shrinks or grows in size depending on how we cut it. Suppose there are thus ways of cutting it unequally such that everyone would get a bigger piece. Rawls would say that if we are rational and nonenvious, we would each prefer an unequal but bigger slice to an equally small slice.

The analogy here is supposed to be about how markets work in the real world. Rawls understood that our income, wealth, and opportunities depend upon capital accumulation. To encourage and enable people to work hard, to use their talents wisely, to put resources to their best use, and so on, at least some degree of economic inequality is necessary.

So far, Rawls would be arguing we should prefer what economists call "Pareto superior" outcomes. A move from situation A to situation B is a "Pareto improvement" if and only if at least one person is made better off without making anyone worse off. More stringently, a situation C is "Pareto optimal" if it is impossible to make at least one person better off without making one person worse off.

But, Rawls might say, while it's obvious we should favor Pareto-superior departures from equality, this still leaves open *which* Pareto-superior departure is the most just. Consider the following three societies (Figure 1). Suppose each has a different set of basic institutions, which tends to lead to different levels of income for different groups. Now let's consider the average income made by three different groups: unskilled workers, skilled workers, and professionals.

| | EGALITARIA | WEALTH-MAXIMIZIA | FAIRNESSARIA |
|---|---|---|---|
| UNSKILLED | $1,000 | $15,000 | $20,000 |
| SKILLED | $1,000 | $75,000 | $50,000 |
| PROFESSIONAL | $1,000 | $500,000 | $100,000 |

*Fig. 1.*

In this example, Rawls would say rational, nonenvious people would prefer to live in either Wealthmaximizia or Fairnessaria. Wealthmaximizia and Fairnessaria are both Pareto superior to Egalitaria. So unless we have some fetish for equality, we'll see both are better than Egalitaria. But this leaves open the question, which society is better, Wealthmaximizia or Fairnessaria?

Rawls would claim we can answer this question by asking what the outcome of a *fair* and *rational* decision procedure would be. Justice is what rational bargainers would agree to under fair conditions. To that end, Rawls developed a thought experiment he called the *Original Position*.

In the Original Position, bargainers come together to choose a set of principles of justice that will in turn be used to determine the institutions they will live under. The bargainers know the basic facts about economics and sociology. They know what human beings are like, and they know there is moderate scarcity. (That is, there are enough resources to ensure everyone gets enough but not enough to ensure that all people get everything they want.) But to make the decision fair—not biased in anyone's favor—the bargainers are placed under a "veil of ignorance." They don't know certain facts about themselves, such as what their conceptions of the good life will be, what religious or philosophical doctrines they will espouse, what position (i.e., status, class) they will be born into, what natural talents they will have, or how valuable their talents will be.

Rawls argues that the parties will choose two basic principles of justice:

1. Each person will be guaranteed an equal set of basic liberties compatible with like liberties for all.

2. Social and economic inequalities are to be arranged so that they are (a) to the greatest advantage of the least advantaged and (b) attached to offices open to all under conditions of fair equality of opportunity.[25]

The second principle is what interests us here. Rawls thought we should pick the institutions that will tend to maximize the total value of the goods (income, leisure, etc.) received by the typical member of the least advantaged *working* class. Rawls called this the "Difference Principle." So, returning to Figure 1 above, the Difference Principle favors Fairnessaria over Wealthmaximizia.

Rawls thought the bargainers in the Original Position would choose the Difference Principle because it guarantees them a higher minimum than under any other possible system. This minimum is sufficient for a decent life. Further, Rawls forbade parties from knowing what percentage of people end up in each income bracket. If we knew that 999 out of 1,000 people in Wealthmaximizia end up making $100,000 or more, we might well take our chances! But because Rawls forbade them this knowledge in the Original Position, the parties are risk averse and choose to ensure the worst they can do is better than under any other set of circumstances.

The Difference Principle is *prioritarian* rather than *egalitarian*. It claims we should give extra weight to the welfare of the least advantaged in the working class. In principle, it allows radical inequality, greater than any the world has ever seen, provided this benefits the least advantaged.

Note that Rawls's second principle of justice applies to people in the least advantaged *working* class, rather than the least advantaged people, period. Rawls thought of justice as a kind of *fair reciprocity*. For Rawls, you have a claim of justice on the "social product" only if you helped produce it. You can claim a slice of the pie only if you helped bake it. So, Rawls would say, if some people are so severely disabled they cannot work, we might owe them duties of natural charity and compassion, but we don't owe them resources as a matter of justice.[26]

Rawls's principles of justice are abstract. It takes a great deal of work and a great deal of social-scientific knowledge to know how to apply them or to know which particular institutions these principles select. Rawls himself thought his principles are best realized by a kind of highly regulated market society, but whether he's right depends upon certain assumptions about how markets and governments work.

Many egalitarians believed Rawls failed to justify departures from economic equality. G. A. Cohen, a prominent Marxist philosopher, complained that Rawls dumbed down his theory of justice to accommodate the bad parts of human nature. Rawls may have been right that it's bad for everyone to be equal but poor, but Cohen thinks that in a truly just society, everyone would be equal and rich. [27]

Rawls's own professed goal was to explain what a "well-ordered society" would look like, and by definition, in a well-ordered society, people care about justice and do what justice requires. [28] Rawls said inequality is justified only if it is necessary to help improve everyone's lot. But, Cohen complained, Rawls's argument for allowing inequality only works if we assume people are selfish and don't care much about justice. Cohen argued that according to Rawls's own premises, in a perfectly just, well-ordered society, all people are committed to achieving justice. This means the most talented people will themselves affirm the view that inequality is justified only if it is necessary to improve everyone's lot. If so, then the most talented people would be willing to work hard for everyone's benefit, not just their own. They would say, "We, the talented, being committed to justice, will simply choose to work hard and make good use of our talents without having to get paid more. Therefore, it's not necessary to pay us more, and so inequality is not necessary or justified." Cohen thought Rawls's Theory of Justice thus isn't really a theory of justice at all. [29] It's not clear Rawls can escape this criticism.

# 6

# *Is Social Justice a Mistake?*

Rawls's Difference Principle is a principle of distributive or social justice. [30] Many classical liberal and libertarian philosophers think the very idea of distributive justice rests on a mistake. They think the concept of social justice is incoherent.

Twentieth-century economist F. A. Hayek sometimes claimed that the term "social justice" is nonsense, a category mistake, like the phrase "green ideas sleep furiously." Ideas can't be green and can't sleep. Similarly, Hayek argued, the "distribution" of wealth in a market society is neither just nor unjust, fair nor unfair. It's neither fair nor unfair that Rawls was born with a silver spoon in his mouth while Nozick wasn't. These aren't things to which the term "justice" properly applies.[31]

Hayek claimed that only the results of intentional human design can properly be called just or unjust. The outcomes of the market are the result of human action, but they are not the result of human design.[32] Like an ecosystem, a market is a spontaneous order. It has a logic of its own. Just as ecosystems tend on their own to maximize biomass, so a market tends toward Pareto efficiency and tends to push the "Pareto frontier" outward. But like an ecosystem, no one is in charge of the market, directing its outcomes. It makes no more sense to complain about the market being unfair than to complain that Mother Nature is cruel to her children.

Nozick, meanwhile, worried the term "distributive justice" is misleading. It makes it sound as though wealth, income, and opportunity are like manna fallen from heaven. As if by magic, the wealth is here! Now we need the government to figure out how to distribute it. But, Nozick said, we didn't find wealth out there to be distributed. We didn't come across a pie in the woods. Wealth gets *made*.

Nozick argued there is no more a distribution of wealth in society than there is a distribution of mates or friends. Consider this: When people make free choices about whom they will associate with, befriend, or have sex with, some people end up with more than others. Some have lots of friends, and some have none. Some have lots of sex with many attractive partners, and some will end up 40-year-old virgins. Nozick thought this is more or less what happens with the market: when people make free choices about what kinds of economic interactions they will have with others, some will end up with more and some with less. So, Nozick asked, if Rawls or Cohen would be repulsed by the idea of redistributing sex or friendship, why would they not be similarly repulsed by the idea of redistributing wealth or the other benefits of economic interactions?[33]

Look back above, in Figure 1, at the distribution of wealth in Egalitaria, Wealthmaximizia, and Fairnessaria. Rawls and most other philosophers ask you, "Which society is most just?" Nozick had a clever answer: "I don't know. I need more information!"

What's missing, Nozick thought, is information about *how* people came to acquire whatever income or wealth they have. The essential problem with egalitarianism, utilitarianism, the Difference Principle, and many other theories of distributive justice is these theories think justice is about matching some preordained pattern of holdings. On the contrary, Nozick said, the paramount issue is not what people have, or whether some have more than others, but whether people came to acquire what they have through just or unjust means.

Nozick said there are two basic kinds of theories of distributive justice:

1. *Patterned theories* of distributive justice hold that the distribution of wealth, income, or opportunity must match some abstract pattern. Here are some examples:

    i. *Egalitarianism*: the distribution of holdings is just if and only if everyone has the same amount.

ii. *Meritocracy*: the distribution of holdings is just if and only if people have wealth in proportion to their merit or desert.

iii. *Rawlsianism*: the distribution of wealth is just if and only if it maximizes the basic goods enjoyed by the representative member of the least advantaged member of the working class.[34]

iv. *Utilitarianism*: the distribution of wealth is just if and only if it maximizes net aggregate happiness.

2. *Historical theories* of distributive justice say the current set of holdings is just if and only if all people came to acquire their holdings the right way.

Nozick gave us only a sketch of what he thought proper historical theory would look like. He called his (sketch of a) theory the "entitlement theory." First, he said, the theory would have some "principle of justice in acquisition," which explains under what conditions people can appropriate unowned resources for themselves. For instance, perhaps people who work productively on unowned land can come to acquire it provided they leave enough and as good for others.

Second, the theory would have some "principle of justice in transfer," which would explain how people can rightfully transfer their holdings to others. (For instance, if I give you my watch, it becomes yours, even if you don't deserve it.)

Third, the theory would have a "principle of justice in rectification," which explains what to do if people violate the first two principles. So, for instance, if I unknowingly buy a stolen watch, perhaps I must return it to its owner.

Nozick said each of these principles would be some complicated truth, and he didn't try to give us all the details. However, he did say a properly historical theory of distributive justice would hold that whatever distribution of holdings arises from an initially just situation through just steps is itself just. That is, if we begin with an initially just scenario, in which people only have what they are entitled to, and then people only transfer their holdings in ways that do not violate others' entitlements, then whatever the end result is (whether people turn out to have equal or unequal wealth) is for that reason just. Nozick said that while Marx's theory of justice can be summarized as "to each according to his needs, from each according to his abilities," his own theory is "from each as they choose; to each as they are chosen." [35]

In principle, Nozick's theory licenses radical inequality. (Remember that, in principle, Rawls's theory does as well.) But note that Nozick did not thereby intend to justify the inequality we actually see in the real world. After all, we haven't been following the entitlement theory. Since the dawn of time, we haven't had a truly free market. Instead, we've had a history of theft, conquest, slavery, and, more recently, crony capitalism, corporatism, rent-seeking, patent trolling, eminent domain abuse, licensing restrictions, restrictions on trade, restrictions on labor mobility, drug wars, and the like, all of which impoverish the worst off and provide many of the wealthy with ill-gotten gains.

So it's a mistake to read Nozick as having claimed it's okay for rich folks like Senator John Kerry or former speaker of the House Nancy Pelosi to live high while people die. Instead, Nozick accepted that to rectify *historical injustice* we might have to redistribute wealth or have government provide welfare services.[36] A perfectly just society would not have such things, Nozick thought, but perhaps the just response to past injustice is to implement them. In the same way, a perfectly just society wouldn't have criminal courts, but that doesn't imply we should get rid of ours.

Nozick argued that patterned theories of distributive justice face a common problem: they seem to be incompatible with granting people even a small amount of liberty. The problem is that *liberty upsets patterns*.

To illustrate, suppose at long last justice is done and your favored pattern of distributive justice comes to be. For the sake of illustration, suppose the pattern is strict equality: everyone has exactly the same amount of wealth as everyone else. Let us call this resulting distribution D1. Let's refer to some other distribution in which one person has $250,000.25 more than everyone else as D2. D2 is unjust by egalitarian lights—after all, only strict equality is just.

Right now, justice is done, and we're at D1. But suppose basketball virtuoso LeBron James offers to let people watch him play basketball provided they each pay him 25 cents per game. Nozick described a (nearly identical) thought experiment in such a way as to make it compatible with socialism. James could play on a community court at an acceptable time using community basketballs. Over the course of a year, a million people watch James play, and thus James now has $250,000.25 more than anyone else: James is $250,000 richer, and everyone else is out a quarter. D2 now obtains.

By egalitarian reasoning, then, the world has been infected with injustice! After all, D2 is an *unacceptable, evil* distribution. It was ruled out from the start. The problem, however, is that D2 came to be because people were using what they were entitled to. At long last, justice was done, and people had what they ought to. However, as people spontaneously exercised their freedom, this over time resulted in a forbidden pattern. But Nozick thought it's absurd to claim that D2 is unjust, and so this shows us that this patterned theory of justice cannot be true.

Nozick generalized that given any pattern principle, people's liberty to use what they are entitled to under the favored pattern will eventually disrupt the pattern. There is thus a conflict between liberty and patterns. What matters is *how* people acquired their goods, not the *pattern* of distribution.

Nozick was not saying that giving people radical libertarian freedom will disrupt a pattern. Rather, he was saying that giving people a tiny amount of economic liberty—the freedom to distribute a single quarter as they see fit—could easily disrupt any pattern over time. Nozick thus worried that to maintain a pattern of holdings would require "continuous interference with individuals' actions and choices." [37] Patterned theories of justice must forbid "capitalist acts among consenting adults." [38]

Hayek and Nozick had a point. It's silly to treat the distribution of wealth like the distribution of cake at a party, and it's silly to focus on who has what without asking how they got it. But there's something to be said on behalf of a weaker view of social justice.

Consider again the question of what justifies the institution of private property in the first place. One could argue that for Locke, ultimately, the institution of private property is good because it systematically enhances our positive liberty. It gets good results. But then we should ask, what count as results good enough to justify the institution? Rawls, Locke, and Nozick all thought some sort of private property institutions are justifiable. They all employed a variety of arguments on behalf of the institutions. All agreed that part of what justifies these institutions is that they tend to produce certain good consequences. But Nozick and Locke had less strict consequentialist standards than Rawls; Rawls thought that to be justified, a private property system must guarantee a higher minimal return to the least advantaged member of the working class than Nozick or Locke did.

By analogy, if Nozick and Rawls were debating the best rules for football, they might make different trade-offs between safety and speed. They both would agree we should play football, but they would disagree about the standards for judging the best set of rules for football. They would disagree about some of the empirical facts. As a result, they would disagree about what the optimal set of rules would be.

Even Hayek and Nozick agreed with these points to some extent. Hayek said one of the main justifications of market institutions—the answer to the question of why we shouldn't scrap them and replace them with something else—is that these institutions tend sufficiently "to enhance the probability that the means needed for the purposes pursued by the different individuals would be available."[39] Like Rawls, Hayek argued that if we were to choose among possible sets of institutions we should choose the one we would be willing to pick if we "knew our initial position in it would be determined purely by chance."[40]

More weakly, Nozick claimed that the system of private property is governed by the "shadow" of the Lockean proviso. It must continue to make people better off with it than without it. As an example, Nozick said, suppose through sheer bad luck all the watering holes dry up except mine, but my watering hole has enough for everyone. In that case, Nozick said, I don't retain full property rights in the water. I can't charge monopoly prices. Perhaps the water might even have to revert back to collective ownership. [41]

Some libertarians complain that all taxation is theft. They uncharitably view advocates of government redistribution as people who believe that government may steal taxpayers' money to feed the poor. Now, perhaps on the final analysis, government taxation will turn out to be theft. But it's important to understand that Rawls and other advocates of redistribution or government-provided social insurance do not see themselves as advocates of theft. Instead, Rawls disagreed with Nozick about what the proper standards are for rendering the institution of private property legitimate. If Nozick were right, then the entitlement theory would be right. In a just world, where people always follow the entitlement theory without fail, a government that taxed me to feed the homeless would indeed be stealing from me. But if Rawls were right, then a regime of property rights would be legitimate only if it tends to satisfy the Difference Principle. If the government taxes me to provide public schools, that does not necessarily count as theft because on Rawls's theory the government is entitled to the money while I am not.

# 7

# *Civil Rights: Freedom of Speech and Lifestyle*

Let's turn now from economic liberties to civil liberties, such as the freedom of lifestyle choice, sexual freedom, the right of assembly, freedom of religion, and the right to free speech. How much freedom should people have in these domains?

John Stuart Mill wrote *On Liberty*, a classic defense of civil liberties, at a time when a few European countries had begun experimenting with democracy. While Mill's father, philosopher James Mill, had thought democracy would solve the problem of tyranny, John Stuart Mill recognized that democracy allowed for the tyranny of the majority. Further, John Stuart Mill believed that social pressure can be as despotic and oppressive as making things illegal. Mill thought that if people were highly intolerant—if they tended to shun everyone who didn't conform to the social and religious norms—this would impede progress almost as much as government-mandated censorship.

Mill was a type of sophisticated utilitarian; that is, he rejected the crude utilitarianism we discussed above. He thought that ultimately the correct *moral code* was whatever code was most conducive to general human happiness. Mill didn't say that every right action had to itself maximize human happiness. Rather, he thought morality as a whole tended to maximize it.

Further, Mill had an expansive notion of happiness. Unlike many utilitarians, he believed happiness was not simply about pleasure. Instead, Mill argued, people could discover what forms part of a happy life through experience (or through learning from others' experience). Mill was highly influenced by the German Romantic movement in poetry and literature. He concluded that the Romantic concept of *Bildung*, autonomous self-development, is the essence of what makes us human and what makes human life worthwhile. [42] A happy life, Mill argued, was an *autonomous, self-directed* life, in which people are the authors of their own actions and in which they rationally affirm their conceptions of what is good or valuable. Thus, Mill rejected crude hedonism, saying, "It is better to be a human being dissatisfied than a pig satisfied; better to be Socrates dissatisfied than a fool satisfied." [43]

*On Liberty* asks, What's the proper sphere of personal autonomy? How much freedom should people have? What may society regulate (whether through law or social disapprobation), and what properly belongs to the individual (free of punishment or censure)? Mill proposed the following solution: we should delimit the sphere of personal liberty at the points where doing so will tend to generate the best overall consequences. He then argued on empirical grounds that this will mean imbuing each individual with an extremely wide sphere of personal liberty.

To illustrate, consider the question of scientific freedom, such as the freedom to pursue new knowledge in physics. Mill would have agreed that such freedom is lost on most of us. Most of us simply don't have the skill or will to do anything with this freedom. Why not, then, allow the government to forbid most of us from writing about physics?

For one, Mill argued, even if some ideas are false or bad, there's tremendous value in grappling with bad ideas. For instance, even though Marxian economics is defunct, I still cover it in some of my courses. Thinking through the mistakes makes the students smarter, and one of them may yet discover a bit of lost insight even in this generally false theory.

Second, Mill argued, we cannot trust government agents to use this power wisely. The power we give them to protect our children may well be used against them instead. When I was in graduate school, I witnessed a law student declare, "This goal of environmental justice is so important that if it takes a KGB to enforce it, so be it. We'll need to make sure the right people run the KGB." But there's no such thing as making sure the right people run the KGB or the board of censors or the Inquisition. People drawn to such jobs (and the power associated with them) will have ends of their own, apart from whatever ends a moral philosopher might wish to press upon them.

Third, even well-meaning agents simply can't know enough about whom to censor and whom to leave alone. No one can reliably predict ahead of time where scientific genius or innovation will come from. Sure, we'd expect the best and the brightest schoolchildren, with the highest test scores, to be the great geniuses. But quite often we're wrong; quite often, some mail clerk somewhere ends up revolutionizing science.

Mill thought similar arguments hold for freedoms of speech, lifestyle, religion, and so on. Mill thought it's no surprise that most scientific progress takes place in free societies or that tolerant commercial hubs are also centers of artistic and cultural progress. Mill argued that if you want good consequences—such as scientific progress, advancement in the arts, cultural progress, peace, and feelings of mutual respect—then you need to allow free speech *regardless* of the consequences. This may sound paradoxical. However, Mill said, the policy of only permitting beneficial speech has no history of being beneficial. The policy of allowing speech only when society judges that speech to be in its best interests has no history of being in society's best interests.

Part of Mill's argument relies upon the idea of *government failure*, a concept I discuss in greater detail below. Mill might say it's one thing to ask how much power we should want to give government over our choices if government were run by competent, benevolent angels. It's quite another to ask how much power it should have if it will be run by real people with ends of their own. Mill worried that if we give government the power to protect us from our own stupidity, government would itself use that power stupidly, excessively, or maliciously against us. He thought the best bet was to give it no such power at all. Sure, that will mean some people will drink themselves to death, but the dangers of trying to stop them are far worse.

Mill convinced many people but not everyone. There's now a large movement on college campuses to suppress speech that makes students uncomfortable or challenges their deepest assumptions. Part of the argument there is that unbridled free speech hurts students' feelings or makes them feel unsafe.

In a far more sophisticated argument along those lines, the contemporary legal theorist Jeremy Waldron recently argued that "hate speech" should be suppressed and regulated. Waldron argued that hate speech can deprive citizens of the assurance that their rights will be protected, render them second-class, and undermine their dignity. [44]

Consider also new paternalistic challenges to Mill. Mill's argument ultimately relies upon an empirical claim—namely, that once we account for government failure, the optimal degree of censorship and control is vanishingly small. But what if he was wrong, and the optimal degree turns out to be higher? In *Nudge*, contemporary legal theorists Cass Sunstein and Richard Thaler defended what they call "libertarian paternalism." (Neither Sunstein nor Thaler is a libertarian, for what that's worth.) Sunstein and Thaler said we should regulate the "choice architecture" of daily life. We should allow people to choose for themselves and even allow them to make self-destructive choices. However, they argue, we should also arrange things so that people are more likely to make good choices.

For instance, Sunstein and Thaler think you should be allowed to eat unhealthy cake instead of healthy fruit. However, certain psychological studies seem to show that people are more likely to choose fruit over cake if the fruit comes first in the cafeteria line. If so, they argue, we might require cafeterias to place the fruit first. (Of course, this isn't really a "libertarian" rule: it coerces sellers, if not consumers.) To take another example: Most people don't save enough for retirement. What if, when they take a new job, the benefits office would by default have them put 15 percent toward retirement unless they explicitly opt out? Here, Sunstein and Thaler said, the worker isn't being forced to be prudent: she can be a grasshopper rather than an ant if she checks the right boxes. But, they say, we know from psychological studies that most people unthinkingly go with the default option. So, they argued, we should make the default options the smarter option while allowing people to make dumb choices if they really want to.

Contemporary political philosopher Sarah Conly goes even further than Sunstein and Thaler. She says recent psychological research has shown that most people are predictably irrational. They are generally not autonomous agents choosing for themselves but rather imperfect agents who do some things autonomously and some things on autopilot. But the problem is that the autopilot often crashes or steers the wrong way. There is little we can do to cultivate higher degrees of rationality. Mill hypothesized that individuals brought up in a liberal, tolerant society would learn to be more rational. Conly responds, Sure, but that's a testable empirical hypothesis, and it's only partly true. Conly argues that in cases where people are predictably short-sighted and imprudent about important matters, the best thing is to force them to make prudent choices. Conly recognizes that any such power might be abused by government, but she doubts that in the final calculation this calls for stripping government of *all* such paternalistic power.

# 8

# *The Scope of Economic Liberty*

Rawls's theory of justice consists of two major principles: a liberty principle and a principle regulating inequalities. What makes Rawls a liberal is that, in his theory, liberty takes priority over questions of distributive justice. For instance, he holds it would be unjust to forbid people from worshipping Zeus even if that somehow improved the welfare of the least advantaged.

Rawls's first principle of justice—the Liberty Principle—requires that every citizen be imbued with a "fully adequate" set of basic rights and liberties. [45] In other, stronger formulations of that principle, Rawls said each citizen must be imbued with the most extensive set of basic liberties compatible with like liberty for all.

Now ask, Which liberties count as "basic" liberties? Just what rights does the first principle of justice include? Rawls responded at first by giving us a list. The first principle includes civil liberties, such as freedoms of conscience, religion, speech, assembly, and lifestyle, as well as sexual freedom. It includes political liberties, such as the right to vote and to run for office and hold office if elected. It includes legal-procedural liberties, such as a right to a fair trial, habeas corpus, due process, and freedom from arbitrary search and seizure. Finally, it includes some economic liberties, such as the right to own personal property and to choose one's own profession.

Notice that Rawls did not include many other economic freedoms—such as freedom of contract, working without a license, or owning productive property—as basic liberties. The Liberty Principle does not protect the people's freedom to make and enter into contracts; to buy and sell goods and services on terms to which all parties consent; to negotiate the terms under which they work; to manage their households as they see fit; to create things for sale, to start, run, and stop businesses; to own factories and businesses; to develop property for productive purposes; to take risks with capital, or to speculate on commodities futures.

Rawls wasn't against you having some such freedoms. After all, he ended up advocating a market economy. However, Rawls claimed we should imbue people with various capitalist economic freedoms only because doing so turns out to be useful for realizing the Difference Principle. According to Rawls, people aren't owed economic liberty as a matter of respect for their autonomous agency or their status as persons. So notice the subtle difference: For Rawls, you are allowed to choose your own religion, even if freedom of religion somehow lowers the average income of the least advantaged. But people are allowed to own factories or stores only if that turns out to be to the advantage of the least advantaged.

In contrast, libertarians and classical liberals hold that economic liberties should be considered on par with civil liberties. They agree with Rawls that imbuing people with such liberties produces good consequences, including for the least advantaged. But they also think people are entitled to economic freedom for the same reasons they're entitled to choose their own religion. It's your life to lead, so you should be able to worship whatever god you want and spend your money however you want, provided you don't infringe upon others' rights.

So why did Rawls disagree? Rawls's major test for whether something counts as a basic liberty is whether it has the right connection to what Rawls called our "two moral powers." The two moral powers are, according to Rawls, (1) a capacity to develop a sense of the good life and (2) a capacity for a sense of justice. The first power, also called "rationality," is the capacity to "have a rational conception of the good— the power to form, revise, and to rationally pursue a coherent conception of values, as based in a view of what gives life and its pursuits their meaning." [46] The second power—also called "reasonableness"—is the capacity to "understand, apply, and cooperate with others on terms of cooperation that are fair." [47]

According to Rawls, these two powers are what make human beings moral beings worthy of special consideration. They are what separate us from, say, the lower animals.

Philosopher Samuel Freeman, perhaps the most important interpreter of Rawls, explained the connection between the *basic* liberties and the moral powers as follows: "What makes a liberty basic for Rawls is that it is an *essential social condition for the adequate development and full exercise of the two powers of moral personality over a complete life.*" [48] Freeman clarified that, for Rawls, liberty is basic only if it is necessary for *all* citizens to have that liberty in order to develop the two moral powers. [49] Since Freeman accepts this view, let's call this the Rawls-Freeman test of basic liberty.

In his recent book *Free Market Fairness*, philosopher John Tomasi argued that Rawls had no principled reason to limit the scope of economic freedom. He thinks most of Rawls's arguments for protecting civil liberties work equally well as arguments for protecting economic liberties. For instance, Rawls argued that freedom of religion is necessary for people to develop their conception of the good life, to be true to themselves and who they really are. Tomasi argued that this is also true of economic liberty. It's not enough, for us to be authors of our own lives, that we choose whether and how to worship; we must also choose how to conduct our economic affairs. Many citizens will not be able to realize their conceptions of the good life without having extensive economic freedom.

Freeman responded by arguing Tomasi misunderstood the Rawls-Freeman test. Sure, Freeman said, maybe it's essential for some entrepreneurs to own a store to realize their conception of the good life. But,

Freeman retorted, not all citizens need such capitalist liberties in order to lead what they see as the good life. [50] For something to be a basic liberty, Freeman claimed, it must be essential to every reasonable person's capacity to develop a sense of the good life or sense of justice. Freeman said Tomasi had at most shown us these capitalist freedoms are essential to many people but had not shown they are essential to all. Thus, Freeman concluded, these capitalist liberties do not pass the Rawls-Freeman test.

Freeman might say to Tomasi that people in Denmark and Switzerland enjoy much more economic liberty than people in Russia. Nevertheless, most Russians develop a sense of justice or a conception of the good life. Indeed, perhaps only a handful of countries allow citizens to have the range of economic liberty Tomasi thinks important, yet despite that, most citizens in those countries can and do develop the two moral powers. This means Tomasi's argument for expanding the list of basic liberties fails: robust economic liberties don't pass the Rawls-Freeman test.

But, as I've pointed out elsewhere, this seems to be a Pyrrhic victory for Rawls and Freeman. The argument for rejecting capitalist freedoms as basic liberties applies equally well against left-liberal freedoms. After all, Rawls and Freeman have thought people have a basic right to extensive freedoms of speech, participation, voting and running for office, and so on. But it is also deeply implausible that it is necessary to have these or other Rawlsian basic liberties in order to develop a sense of justice or a conception of the good life. Again, people in Denmark and Switzerland enjoy much more civil liberty than people in Russia or China. But, nevertheless. most Russians can and do develop a sense of justice and conception of the good life. At best, a small handful of countries afford their citizens the full scope of Rawlsian basic liberties. However, in the overwhelming majority of the unjust countries, the overwhelming majority of people do develop (and most of the rest *could* develop) a sense of justice and a conception of the good, despite lacking these basic liberties or despite not having the liberties be protected at the level Freeman and Rawls have believed they should.

In fact, it seems very little liberty is strictly necessary for the typical person (let alone *all* people, as Freeman would have it) to develop the two moral powers. So it's not clear *anything* passes the Rawls-Freeman test.

Let's take a step back and reflect on the upshot of this debate. Most classical liberal and libertarian thinkers believe economic rights aren't merely a useful institution, an institution that tends to generate good consequences. Instead, they argue such rights are necessary because they show respect for people.

I agree with them. However, at the end of the day, consequences still matter. A great deal of the debate about the scope of economic liberty concerns what will happen if we draw the line here or there. Marxists think extensive capitalist freedoms would mean the poor get poorer while the rich get richer. In turn, the rich will exploit the poor for their own ends. Libertarians think extensive capitalist freedoms will mean that everyone, the poor and the rich, get richer. Deontological considerations only get us so far. If, as Marxists claim, capitalist freedoms generally lead to disaster, we'd be hard-pressed to advocate them. If capitalism tended to immiserate us, then libertarian justice would be a kind of curse.

# 9

# *Government Authority and Legitimacy*

A government is a subset of a society that claims a monopoly (over certain people in a geographic area) on the legitimate use of coercion and that has coercive power sufficient to maintain that monopoly. [51] Governments claim a monopoly right to create and impose rules, and they also assert that citizens have a *moral duty* to abide by these rules.

We're used to having governments, so we tend to presume they're good things to have. But it's worthwhile being puzzled at the commonplace. Consider: Monopolies are generally bad—we don't want Walmart to become a monopoly retailer, after all. So why do so many people think we should have monopolies on rule-making power? Also, as I noted in the introduction, governments generally claim the right to do things no private individual would have the right to do. If Vani cannot forbid you from drinking soda, why might a government be able to? (Or is it also wrong for governments to do so?)

Governments characteristically claim two special moral powers:

1.  The permission to create and enforce rules over certain people within a geographic area.

2.  The power to create in others a *moral obligation* to obey those rules.

Generally, political philosophers use the word "legitimacy" to refer to the first moral power while they use the word "authority" to refer to the second. [52] (However, be careful when reading political philosophy: The use of the technical terms "legitimacy" and "authority" isn't exactly standardized. Some authors use the terms differently.)

By definition, a government is legitimate just in case it is permissible for that government to stand and to create, issue, and coercively enforce rules. This leaves open a few questions that every theory of government legitimacy will have to settle:

1.  Does any government in fact have legitimacy? (What determines whether a government has legitimacy?)

2. What is the *scope* of government legitimacy? That is, over what issues may a government create rules? For instance, liberals standardly believe it is outside the scope of government legitimacy to forbid you from having sex with another consenting adult.

3. *How* may government enforce the rules? Few people think governments may execute lawbreakers upon their first minor offense. Instead, there are many complicated questions about what is the best and most just way to enforce the rules.

4. What is the *range* of a government? That is, over which people does a particular government permissibly create and enforce rules? So suppose Canada and the United States go to war and both countries claim to draft me

into their armies. The average American just concludes it's obvious the U.S. government may force me to go to war while the Canadian government may not. But perhaps that's not so obvious. A full theory of government legitimacy has to settle questions about what determines the rightful boundaries of a government's legitimate rule. As we'll see below, that's hard to do.

By definition, a government is authoritative (or "has authority") over certain people just in case those people have a moral duty to obey that government's laws, edicts, and commands. Similar questions arise for authority as do for legitimacy:

1. Does any government actually have authority? (What determines whether a government has authority?)

2.  What is the proper scope of government authority?

3.  How strong is the duty to obey?

4.  What is the proper range of government authority?

To clarify the difference, legitimacy makes it okay for the police to arrest you. Authority makes it wrong for you to resist them when they try to arrest you. In short, "legitimacy" refers to the moral permission to coerce, while "authority" refers to a moral power that induces in others a duty to submit and obey.

Importantly, to say a government has authority is to say it has the power to *create* obligations where previously there were none. By definition, if government has authority over a person, then when the government commands that person to do something, she has a moral duty to do it *because* the government says so. So consider that I have a preexisting moral duty not to kill my neighbor. My government also forbids me to do so. However, it seems that the reason I have a moral duty not to kill my neighbor is not that my government told me not to. Rather, it's wrong independent of what the government commands. If the government gave me special dispensation to kill my neighbor, it would remain wrong to do so. The government did not create my duty not to kill, and it cannot relieve me of it.

On the other hand, my government also commands me to pay it about a third of my income in tax. Here, if I have a duty to pay that tax, this duty exists only because my government created it. If the government rescinded the command, the duty to pay would disappear. If the government decided to change the duty—say, to require only a quarter of my income—then my duty would change.

Legitimacy and authority are independent moral properties. It's logically possible for a government to have legitimacy but lack authority. In that case, a government could permissibly create and enforce rules, but we would have no obligation to *obey* those rules. (To be more precise, we'd have no duty to obey the rules because the government orders us to do so, though we might have independent reasons to obey the rules.) So, for instance, one might hold that governments may permissibly tax citizens but still hold that citizens have no duty to comply and could feel free to engage in tax evasion if they can get away with it.

This may seem odd to the lay reader, who probably presumes that legitimacy and authority come and go together. However, following contemporary philosopher A. John Simmons's seminal work on political obligation, the standard view among political philosophers who work on this topic now seems to be that some governments have legitimacy but none have authority.[53] That is, some governments permissibly create and enforce laws, but no one has a duty to obey the government. Most laypeople believe we have a duty to obey the state—even when it issues mildly or moderately unjust commands—but it seems that the typical philosopher who writes on authority concludes we have no duty to obey. At the least, the claim that we have a duty to obey the law or defer to the state is extremely controversial among political philosophers.

The main and most popular argument for why some governments might be legitimate is consequentialist. The argument is outlined as follows:

1.  We have either some sort of anarchy or some sort of government.

2. Anarchy would be disastrous, but life under certain forms of government would be pretty good.

3. Therefore, we should have government.

Consider, as an example, a variation on 17th-century philosophers Thomas Hobbes and John Locke's arguments for the state. By default, it seems implausible that anyone would have permission to create and enforce rules over others. Or, Locke would say, by default, we'd presume that every person has the same liberty to enforce rights and punish rights violations. However, they both think that without a central, monopolistic enforcement agency, things will go badly. Hobbes believed that in the absence of government, life would be "nasty, poor, brutish, and short."[54] People would not be able to trust each other and would turn to preying upon each other preemptively. Locke was less pessimistic; he held there would instead be severe "inconveniences." [55] Many rights violations would go unpunished. It would be difficult to enforce rights violations in a fair and impartial way. People would be biased in their own favor. They might come to blows or to war as a result.

Hobbes and Locke both then argued that certain forms of government would solve these problems. Of course, these kinds of consequentialist arguments depend upon consequences, and so it matters a great deal what the facts are. If it turns out empirically that some form of anarchism performs roughly as well as governmentalism, then these kinds of arguments would fail. [56]

Along those lines, one of the most common economic arguments for the legitimacy of the state is the "public-goods argument." A "public good" is defined as a good that is nonrivalrous and nonexcludable. To say a good is nonrivalrous is to say that when one person enjoys or uses it, this does not diminish another person's ability to enjoy or use it. To say a good is nonexcludable is to say there is no way to provide the good for one person without providing it for others. For instance, suppose an asteroid is about to hit the Earth. If Bill Gates pays $50 billion to launch an expedition to destroy the asteroid, he doesn't merely save himself. He saves *everyone*. Some common purported examples of public goods include flood-control systems, lighthouses, roads, air quality, and national defense.

The public-goods argument for the state goes as follows:

1. There are certain public goods that are vital to leading a decent life.

2. The market will tend to underprovide those public goods.

3. The government will tend to provide them at roughly the right level.

4. Therefore, we ought to have government.

Notice that premise 1 is a normative claim, while premises 2 and 3 are empirical claims. So for the argument to go through, it's vital to establish as a philosophical point that there are certain goods so valuable that it would be worth creating a state to get them. Premises 2 and 3 are empirical, social-scientific claims. The main subargument for premise 2 is that because the goods in question are nonexcludable, people will try to "free ride" on others if those others provide them. The worry is that if all people think to themselves, "I'll get the benefit regardless of whether I pay for it," then no one will pay for it and no one will get the benefit. [57]

Now let's turn to the question of government authority. To say a government has authority over you (in some domain) is to say that if that government creates a law or issues a command (say, through some sort of legal process), you have to obey that law or command. Over the past 2,500 years, philosophers have produced a wide range of theories attempting to explain why some governments might have some such authority. However, it appears that each of these theories fails, which is why skepticism about government authority is now the dominant position. I don't have space here to review each of these theories, but I will cover a few of the most prominent.

Perhaps the most common theory is that government has authority because we have in some way *consented* to its authority. Most of us were told in grade school that democracy rests on the consent of the governed. Socrates (as portrayed by Plato in *Crito*) and Locke both argued that in one way or another, we've consented to the government's rule in the form of a "social contract." Consider: I have a contract with Georgetown University. In exchange for salary and benefits, I agree to follow certain commands, such as their command that I teach certain courses. Perhaps our relationship to government is like that: we agree to obey and pay taxes in exchange for protection and social insurance.

The problem, though, is that our relationship to government doesn't appear consensual at all. Genuinely consensual relationships have certain features.[58] Recently, I consented to buy a Fender American Deluxe Telecaster. All of the following were true:

A.  I performed an act that signified my consent. In this case, I ordered the guitar from a dealer.

The outcome—that I lost money but gained a Telecaster—would not have occurred but for my performing the act that signified consent.

B.  I was not forced to perform that act: I had a reasonable way to avoid doing it.

C.  Had I explicitly said, "I refuse to buy a Fender Telecaster at that price!" the exchange never would have taken place.

D.  The dealer was not entitled to take my money unless it sent me the guitar: it had to hold up its end of the bargain.

Had any of these conditions failed to obtain, it would not have been a consensual transaction. Suppose, instead of A, the dealer sent me the guitar and took my money, even though I never placed an order. That's not consent: that's theft. Suppose, instead of

B, the dealer put a gun to my head and told me I must buy the guitar or die. That's not consent: it's robbery. Suppose, instead of C, my dealer sometimes called me and asked whether I needed anything. Suppose I said to him, "I don't need or want a Telecaster." Now suppose he then sent it to me anyway. That's not consent: that's an unwanted gift. Suppose instead of D, the dealer took my money but kept the guitar. That's not consent: that's fraud or breach of contract.

Our relationship with government looks much more like these cases of theft, robbery, unwanted gifts, or fraud and breach of contract than it does like a case of a consensual relationship. Regardless of whether you vote or participate or consent, or what you say or do, your government will impose rules, regulations, restrictions, benefits, and taxes upon you. Your actions make no difference.

Further, you have no reasonable way of opting out of government control. Governments control all the habitable land, so you have no reasonable way to escape government rule. (You can't even move to Antarctica: the governments of the world forbid you to live there.) At most, a small minority of us—those who have the financial means and the legal permission to emigrate—can choose *which* government will rule us. Even that—choosing which government will rule you—does not signify real consent. Imagine a group of men say to a woman, "You must marry one of us or drown in the ocean, but we will let you choose whom you marry." When she picks a husband, she does not consent to being married. She has no real choice. [59]

Further, even if you actively dissent, the government will just impose the rules upon you anyway. Suppose you smoke marijuana. You dissent from marijuana-criminalization laws and believe it is deeply immoral to throw people in jail for possessing marijuana. The government will still just throw you in jail for possession. This is unlike a consensual transaction, where saying no means no. For the government, your no doesn't matter.

Finally, governments require you to abide by their rules and will force you to pay taxes even if they do not do their part and keep up their end of the transaction. So, for instance, if the government fails to provide adequate education or fails to protect you, it will still force you to pay taxes and to comply with its rules. As contemporary philosopher Michael Huemer notes, the U.S. Supreme Court has repeatedly ruled that the government has no duty to protect individual citizens. Suppose you call the police to alert them that an intruder is in your house, but the police never bother to dispatch someone to help you, and as a result the intruder rapes you. The government still requires you to pay taxes for the protection services it chose not to deploy on your behalf. [60]

No government, not even a democratic one, is grounded on anything like a contractual or consensual relationship. Philosophers have thus tried to defend other kinds of theories of authority. Some argued that governments are authoritative not because we, in fact, consent to them but because we *would* consent to them if we were reasonable and fully informed. Others have argued that we have duties of fair play, reciprocity, or gratitude, and to discharge such duties we need to obey the law. I won't review these theories here, but an interested reader can see the Recommended Readings for more.

**10**

# What Counts as "Society"?

We've been tossing around the word "society" freely. Many philosophers follow suit. For instance, Rawls stated that a theory of justice is meant to evaluate the "basic structure of society," by which he meant that society's institutions. He said, "Society is a cooperative venture for mutual gain." [61] Many philosophers argue we have obligations of civic virtue, to promote the common good of society. [62] When egalitarians complain about inequalities of wealth, they mean inequalities within a society. Cultural relativists hold that moral truths vary from society to society. Laypeople claim we have a debt to society. And so on.

But what counts as a society? Where does one society stop and another begin? How sharp are the boundaries? Am I a member of exactly one society or many? If I'm a member of many societies, then which one matters the most for questions of justice?

Most people just assume, without reflection, that their society consists of all their fellow citizens or residents in whatever nation-state they happen to live. But that's a problematic assumption. If Rawls was right that a society is a cooperative venture for mutual gain, then the boundaries of my society don't equal the U.S. national borders. My sphere of cooperation is both broader and narrower than that. Consider that tens of millions of people in some way contributed to producing the computer upon which I now type, while tens of millions of other people contributed to produce the food I'll eat for lunch later. Some of these people are American, but most are not. Likewise, in my day-to-day life, I interact with a small number of people, many of whom are American but many of whom are not.

*Nationalism* is the claim that we have a special moral tie to fellow members of our nation-state. Nationalists hold that the fact we happen to be citizens of different nation-states is morally important. They think we owe more to our fellow citizens than we owe to others. You can see examples of nationalism in, for instance, calls to "buy American" or alternatively in the way most Americans remain nonplussed when the American military kills civilians in other countries.

Nationalism is the view that we should treat all the members of our nation-states as part of an extended family. Commonsense morality holds that we do not have to be impartial among all other people. In commonsense thinking, not only *may* I show special preference for my family and friends over strangers, but I *should*. Few people would think it right for me to refuse to give my wife a ride to the airport just because I find some stranger needs the ride slightly more.

If nationalism were true, then this would explain why, for example, Sweden may spend huge sums promoting the welfare of its quite wealthy "lower" classes while more or less ignoring the significantly greater suffering of the world's desperate poor. Or if more extreme forms of nationalism were true, then it would explain why governments may kill, exploit, or impoverish innocent civilians of other countries to benefit their own citizens even when the costs to foreign citizens greatly exceed the benefits to their own citizens.

There are at least two alternatives to nationalism. *Cosmopolitanism* is the thesis that from the standpoint of justice, everyone everywhere counts equally. Cosmopolitans hold that membership in a nation-state is for the most part morally arbitrary. Other citizens are not like friends or family but strangers. I have no special connection to people in California as opposed to Ontario. Domestic governments must not treat the citizens of foreign nations as if their lives were less valuable.

Another alternative is *localism*. Localism holds that we do indeed have special ties to a community (larger than our sphere of friends and family), but this community is our *local* community. For instance, many people now advocate buying locally rather than buying American because they think we owe it to producers in our own towns and neighboring towns to purchase their products rather than those of competitors from farther away.

As a rule, if not as a matter of logical necessity, economists, classical liberals, and libertarians tend to be cosmopolitans. Most left-liberal philosophers are nationalists, though many are cosmopolitan. Left-leaning communitarians tend to be localist, while conservatives tend to be nationalists. We can speculate why this might be so. Perhaps it's a difference in psychology rather than philosophy. As moral psychologist Jonathan Haidt says, libertarians and conservatives differ in whether they regard loyalty as a foundational moral concept. [63] Perhaps it's in part because economics tells us not to treat state borders as magic—there's no real difference between trade across state borders versus the county line—and libertarians are more likely than conservatives to apply economic reasoning to moral matters.

# 11

# *Why Political Philosophy Needs Political Economy*

Consider the following argument:

1. Government ought to promote human welfare and is licensed to do whatever it takes to do so.

2. If government ought to promote human welfare and is licensed to do whatever it takes to

do so, then we should have a welfare state that guarantees through legal means that no one falls below a particular standard of welfare.

3.  Therefore, we should have a welfare state that guarantees through legal means that no one falls below a particular standard of welfare.

Suppose for the sake of argument that premise 1 is correct. Even with that charitable assumption, the argument is unsound. The problem is that premise 2 is questionable. We would need to check whether welfare states actually improve welfare best, in the long run, compared to the other institutional arrangements. If we care about welfare, we wouldn't take that for granted. We'd check to make sure.

Political philosophers and students of political philosophy often fail to check to make sure. Instead, they commit what I like to call the Fallacy of Direct

Governmentalism. The Fallacy of Direct Governmentalism is the mistake of presuming that if something is valuable, then it (1) ought to be promoted by government and (2) ought to be promoted by government in a direct manner.

These are two separate mistakes. First, even if you conclude that something is valuable, it doesn't automatically follow that government should try to promote it at all. It's an open question whether that's a job for government. Whether government gets the job of promoting that value depends in part on whether we may rightly use coercion to produce that value. (For instance, I think Swedish progressive death metal is high art, but I don't think we may use coercion to ensure we generate more of it.) It also depends at least in part on whether government is the most effective institution for promoting that value. It might not be.

Second, even if you conclude that government should get the job, it has two ways of promoting the value: directly and indirectly. For example, suppose you think the government ought to ensure the economy grows. It could attempt to do this directly by subsidizing new corporations, offering grants to businesses, or spending money for the purpose of stimulus. Or it could try to do it indirectly by maintaining a basic institutional framework (such as the rule of law, constitutional representative democracy, courts, and property rights) under which people will be incentivized to act in ways that spontaneously lead to growth. It's an empirical, social-scientific question which mix of direct and indirect methods works best to achieve this goal. We should not just presume direct methods work better than indirect. Indeed, in this case, economic research tends to find that indirect methods are usually best.

Rawls, in some parts of his writings, thought it's useful to put aside these questions of political economy. He said we should instead just imagine that institutions always accomplish their intended ends. [64] But with all due respect to Rawls, that's probably the last thing we'd want to do if we want to think carefully about institutions. Instead, we'd never assume institutions accomplish their intended ends but carefully study what factors determine how institutions would work.

Imagine if engineers were designing cars and said, "We're doing *ideal* car theory. So let's imagine that the components accomplish their intended ends." In that case, the engineers might well put the seatbelt on the outside of the car or put the rearview mirror in the trunk. "Sure, that wouldn't work in the real world, but we're imagining the components accomplish their intended ends." Really, once we take Rawls' advice, all bets are off. We might as well say the best way to achieve justice is to sing "Kum Ba Yah" at summer camp.

More seriously, think about the question of legal guarantees. There's a difference between guaranteeing in the sense of rendering inevitable—as when an economist says rampant protectionism guarantees lower economic growth—and guaranteeing in the sense of expressing a firm commitment to achieve some goal through government action—as when George W. Bush guaranteed no child will be left behind. Clearly, a guarantee in the second sense need not be a guarantee in the first. Indeed, it's possible that a legal guarantee that the government will accomplish some goal is the very thing that guarantees the goal won't be accomplished. For instance, if the government legally guaranteed that every American would have a minimum real income of

$1 million, this would hurt rather than help Americans. In that regime, few people would choose to work, and so there would be insufficient taxes to pay for the guaranteed basic income.

Contemporary economist and political scientist Michael Munger has a thought experiment that parodies a common mistake people make when reasoning about institutions. Imagine the state fair decides to hold a "Big Pretty Pig" contest. There end up being only two entries. While there are lots of big pigs and plenty of pretty pigs, few pigs are both big and pretty. The judge takes a long look at the first pig and exclaims, "My God, that's one ugly pig! You know what, let's just give the prize to the second one." The judge's mistake is clear: the second pig might be even uglier. The judge should look before deciding. It's an obvious mistake, but many economists, political scientists, and philosophers make this same mistake when they judge institutions. They complain about how ugly some institutions are in practice and then say we should go with their favored alternatives instead. But they fail to examine whether their favored alternatives are even uglier.

For instance, consider the following argument a left-liberal might make:

1. There is a market failure in this sector of the economy. [65]

2. In principle, government regulation could fix the problem.

3. Therefore, we should empower the government to fix the problem.

The problem with this argument is that just as markets can and do fail, so governments can and do fail. It's one thing to argue that in principle, a fully informed and well-motivated government could correct a market failure. It's another thing to argue that a real-life government will actually correct a market failure. When introductory economics textbooks call for government intervention, they stipulate that the governments in question know how to correct market failures and will use their power to do so. In the real world, we don't get to stipulate governments are like that. That could make all the difference in what we want real-life governments to do.

This is a primer on political philosophy, not political economy. However, my final goal here is just to warn readers to take political economy seriously. It's not possible to make a final recommendation about what institutions we should favor without understanding how these institutions function. A careful thinker will always consider how to balance market and government failures, as well as market and government successes. [66] Philosophy can help us think more clearly about politics, but it can also tempt us into believing we can solve all the world's problems from the armchair with a few clever arguments. Thus, my final recommendation is that you, the reader, don't stop here. Learn basic economics, political science, and sociology as well.

# *Endnotes*

1. Douglass North, *Institutions, Institutional Change, and Economic Performance* (New York: Cambridge University Press, 1990), p. 3.

2. For an overview, see Dennis Chong, "Degrees of Rationality in Politics," in *The Oxford Handbook of Political Psychology*, ed. Leonie Huddy, David O. Sears, and Jack S. Levy (New York: Oxford University Press, 2013), pp. 96–129.

3. For example, see Aaron Ross Powell, ed., *Arguments for Liberty* (Washington, D.C.: Cato Institute, 2014), which illustrates how libertarians could accept any of at least 10 different moral theories.

4. See Gerald Gaus, *Political Concepts and Political Theories* (Boulder, CO: Westview Press, 2000).

5. John Rawls, *A Theory of Justice* (Cambridge, MA: Harvard University Press, 1971), p. 4.

6. See Michael Clemens, "Economics and Emigration: Trillion-Dollar Bills on the Sidewalk?" *Journal of Economic Perspectives* 23 (2011): pp. 83–106.

7. Economists say that a change from the status quo is Pareto superior just in case at least one person is made better off without making anyone else worse off. In the real world, many changes help some people but hurt others. Economists are thus interested in Kaldor-Hicks efficiency. A change from the status quo is Kaldor-Hicks efficient if and only if it helps some and hurts others but the gain to the winners is higher than the loss to the losers. In this case, the winners could compensate the losers for their losses. Thus, a Kaldor-Hicks-superior change is potentially a Pareto-superior change.

8. Robert Nozick, *Anarchy, State, and Utopia* (New York: Basic Books, 1974), p. 41.

9. Ibid.

10. Wesley Newcomb Hohfeld, "Fundamental Legal Conceptions as Applied in Judicial Reasoning," *Yale Law Journal* 23 (1913): pp. 16–59.

11. Isaiah Berlin, "Two Concepts of Liberty," in Isaiah Berlin, *The Proper Study of Mankind*, ed. Henry Hardy, Roger Hausheer, and Noel Annan (New York: Farrar, Straus, and Giroux, 1997), p. 168.

12. Ibid., p. 169.

13. G. A. Cohen, *Self-Ownership, Freedom, and Equality* (New York: Cambridge University Press, 1995), p. 58.

14. John Stuart Mill, *On Liberty* (Indianapolis, IN: Hackett Publishing, 1978).

15. Gerald Gaus, "Property," in *The Oxford Handbook of Political Philosophy*, ed. David Estlund (New York: Oxford University Press, 2012), p. 96.

16. Jean-Jacques Rousseau, *The Major Political Writings of Jean-Jacques Rousseau*, trans. John T. Scott (Chicago: University of Chicago Press, 2012), p. 91.

17. John Locke, *Second Treatise of Government* (Indianapolis, IN: Hackett Publishing, 1980), p. 21.

18. See Angus Maddison's historical GDP/capita data, available here: http://www.ggdc.net/maddison/Maddison.htm. See also Angus Maddison, *Contours of the World Economy, 1–2030 AD: Essays in Macroeconomic History* (New York: Oxford University Press, 2003).

19. http://aspe.hhs.gov/poverty/15poverty.cfm. Author's calculations.

20. Maddison, *Contours of the World Economy, 1–2030 AD*.

21. David Schmidtz and Jason Brennan, *A Brief History of Liberty* (Oxford: Wiley-Blackwell, 2010), p. 122; and http://www.ggdc.net/maddison/Maddison.htm

22. David Schmidtz, "The Institution of Property," *Social Philosophy and Policy* 11 (1994): pp. 42–62.

23. Garrett Hardin, "The Tragedy of the Commons," *Science* 162 (1968): pp. 1243–48.

24. I owe this way of characterizing Rawls to David Schmidtz, *Elements of Justice* (New York: Cambridge University Press, 2006), pp. 187–88, 219.

25. Rawls 1971, p. 60.

26. For a sustained critique of Rawls on this point, see Martha Nussbaum, *Frontiers of Justice* (Cambridge, MA: Harvard University Press, 2007).

27. G. A. Cohen, *Rescuing Justice and Equality* (New York: Oxford University Press, 2009).

28. Rawls 1971, pp. 453–55.

29. See Cohen 2009; G. A. Cohen, *Why Not Socialism?* (Princeton, NJ: Princeton University Press, 2008).

30. Principles of distributive justice are meant to explain what the proper "distribution" of wealth, income, or other basic goods should be. Principles of "social justice" are a subset of principles of distributive justice. Advocates of social justice believe that distributive justice requires some sort of special emphasis on the poor. So, for example, a meritocrat believes people should have income in proportion to their desert or merit. The meritocrat would thus accept a principle of distributive justice but not a principle of social justice.

31. F. A. Hayek, *Law, Legislation, and Liberty, Volume II: The Mirage of Social Justice* (Chicago: University of Chicago Press, 1978).

32. Adam Ferguson, *An Essay on the History of Civil Society* (New York: Cambridge University Press, 1996), p. 119.

33. Nozick 1974, pp. 150–59. Cohen 1995, pp. 229–44, takes the bait and wonders about redistributing eyes. Cecile Fabre, *Whose Body Is It Anyway?* (New York: Oxford University Press, 2006), argues for the forced redistribution of eyes and other organs.

34. Strictly speaking, Rawls doesn't say this. For him, the Difference Principle is subordinate to the Liberty Principle and the principle of fair equality of opportunity. Strictly speaking, Rawls's view is that we should try to realize the Difference Principle as much as possible but must treat the Liberty Principle and principle of fair opportunity as side constraints.

35. Nozick 1974, p. 160.

36. Ibid., pp. 151–52, 344n2.

37. Ibid., p. 166.

38. Ibid., p. 163.

39. F. A. Hayek, *New Studies in Philosophy, Politics, Economics, and the History of Ideas* (Chicago: University of Chicago Press, 1986), pp. 132–34. I owe the discovery of this often-overlooked line to John Tomasi.

40. Ibid., p. 132.

41. Nozick 1974, p. 180.

42. Nicholas Capaldi, *John Stuart Mill: A Biography* (New York: Cambridge University Press, 2004).

43. John Stuart Mill, *Utilitarianism* (Indianapolis, IN: Hackett Publishing, 2002), p. 10.

44. Jeremy Waldron, *The Harm in Hate Speech* (Cambridge, MA: Harvard University Press, 2014).

45. Rawls 1996, pp. 5–6.

46. Samuel Freeman, *Rawls* (New York: Routledge Press, 2009), p. 54.

47. Ibid.

48. Ibid., p. 55. Italics in original.

49. http://bleedingheartlibertarians.com/2012/06/can-economic-liberties-be-basic-liberties/.

50. Ibid.

51. Paraphrasing Gregory Kavka, "Why Even Morally Perfect People Would Need Government," *Social Philosophy and Policy* 12 (1995): pp. 1–18; here p. 2.

52. David Estlund, *Democratic Authority* (Princeton, NJ: Princeton University Press, 2007), p. 2.

53. See, e.g., A. John Simmons, "Philosophical Anarchism," in *For and against the State: New Philosophical Readings*, ed. John T. Sanders and A. John Simmons (Boulder, CO: Rowman and Littlefield, 1996), pp. 19–30. Note that Simmons does not use the words authority and legitimacy the way I do, as the definitions I use became standard later in the literature. For a survey showing how untenable most accounts of political obligation are, see M. B. E. Smith, "The Duty to Obey the Law," in *Companion to the Philosophy of Law and Legal Theory*, ed. D. Patterson (Oxford: Blackwell, 1996). See also Arthur

Isak Applbaum, "Legitimacy without the Duty to Obey," *Philosophy and Public Affairs* 38 (2010): pp. 216–39.

54. Thomas Hobbes, *Leviathan* (Indianapolis, IN: Hackett Publishing, 1994), p. 78.

55. Locke 1980, pp. 72–73.

56. For a sustained argument along those lines, see Michael Huemer, *The Problem of Political Authority* (New York: Palgrave MacMillan, 2013).

57. For a counterargument, see David Schmidtz, *The Limits of Government: An Essay on the Public Goods Argument* (Boulder, CO: Westview Press, 1990).

58. The next few paragraphs incorporate material from Brennan 2016, pages to be determined.

59. For a further refutation of consent theories of political legitimacy, see Huemer 2013, pp. 20–58; Christopher Heath Wellman and John Simmons, *Is There a Duty to Obey the Law?* (New York: Cambridge University Press, 2006), pp. 116–18.

60. Huemer 2013, pp. 32–33. Huemer cites three separate recent cases in which the Supreme Court held that the government has no duties to individual citizens, but only to the public at large.

61. Rawls 1971, p. 4.

62. For example, Richard Dagger, *Civic Virtues* (New York: Oxford University Press, 1997).

63. See Jonathan Haidt, *The Righteous Mind* (New York: Vintage, 2013).

64. John Rawls, *Justice as Fairness: A Restatement* (Cambridge, MA: Harvard University Press, 2001), pp. 137–38.

65. A market fails whenever it doesn't reach full Pareto efficiency. In the real world, markets are hardly ever perfect and so "fail" all the time. Most "failures" are not severe, and so the term "market failure" is misleading. Similar remarks apply to the term "government failure."

66. For example, Elinor Ostrom, *Governing the Commons* (New York: Cambridge University Press, 1990).

# *Recommended Readings*

**John Rawls,** *Justice as Fairness: A Restatement.* A short and concise summary of Rawls's final theory. Rawls set out to systematize and defend left-liberal ideals. He emerged as the dominant political philosopher of the past 50 years. Many philosophers now regard Rawls as the baseline from which departures must be justified.

**David Schmidtz,** *Elements of Justice.* In this easy-to-read, remarkable book, Schmidtz helps readers sort through some of the most perplexing ideas about justice, freedom, reciprocity, equality, and desert.

**Michael Huemer,** *The Problem of Political Authority.* Huemer surveys every major theory of government authority and finds the theories wanting. A stunning defense of anarchism on the basis of commonsense morality.

# About the Author

Jason Brennan (Ph.D., 2007, University of Arizona) is the Robert J. and Elizabeth Flanagan Family Associate Professor of Strategy, Economics, Ethics, and Public Policy at the McDonough School of Business at Georgetown University. He is the author of *Markets without Limits*, with Peter Jaworkski (Routledge Press, 2015); *Compulsory Voting: For and Against*, with Lisa Hill (Cambridge University Press, 2014); *Why Not Capitalism?* (Routledge Press, 2014); *Libertarianism: What Everyone Needs to Know* (Oxford University Press, 2012); *The Ethics of Voting* (Princeton University Press, 2011); and, with David Schmidtz, *A Brief History of Liberty* (Wiley-Blackwell, 2010). He is currently writing *Against Politics*, under contract with Princeton University Press, and, with Bas Van der Vossen, *Global Justice as Global Freedom: Why Global Libertarianism is the Humane Solution to World Poverty*, under contract with Oxford University Press.

# *Libertarianism.org*

Liberty. It's a simple idea and the linchpin of a complex system of values and practices: justice, prosperity, responsibility, toleration, cooperation, and peace. Many people believe that liberty is the core political value of modern civilization itself, the one that gives substance and form to all the other values of social life. They're called libertarians.

Libertarianism.org is the Cato Institute's treasury of resources about the theory and history of liberty. The book you're holding is a small part of what Libertarianism.org has to offer. In addition to hosting classic texts by historical libertarian figures and original articles from modern-day thinkers, Libertarianism.org publishes podcasts, videos, online introductory courses, and books on a variety of topics within the libertarian tradition.

# *Cato Institute*

Founded in 1977, the Cato Institute is a public policy research foundation dedicated to broadening the parameters of policy debate to allow consideration of more options that are consistent with the principles of limited government, individual liberty, and peace. To that end, the Institute strives to achieve greater involvement of the intelligent, concerned lay public in questions of policy and the proper role of government.

The Institute is named for Cato's Letters, libertarian pamphlets that were widely read in the American Colonies in the early 18th century and played a major role in laying the philosophical foundation for the American Revolution.

Despite the achievement of the nation's Founders, today virtually no aspect of life is free from government encroachment. A pervasive intolerance for individual rights is shown by government's arbitrary intrusions into private economic transactions and its disregard for civil liberties. And while freedom around the globe has notably increased in the past several decades, many countries have moved in the opposite direction, and most governments still do not respect or safeguard the wide range of civil and economic liberties.

To address those issues, the Cato Institute undertakes an extensive publications program on the complete spectrum of policy issues. Books, monographs, and shorter studies are commissioned to examine the federal budget, Social Security, regulation, military spending, international trade, and myriad other issues. Major policy conferences are held throughout the year, from which papers are published thrice yearly in the *Cato Journal*. The Institute also publishes the quarterly magazine *Regulation*.

In order to maintain its independence, the Cato Institute accepts no government funding. Contributions are received from foundations, corporations, and individuals, and other revenue is generated from the sale of publications. The Institute is a nonprofit, tax-exempt, educational foundation under Section 501(c)3 of the Internal Revenue Code.

CATO INSTITUTE
1000 Massachusetts Ave., N.W.
Washington, D.C. 20001
www.cato.org

CPSIA information can be obtained
at www.ICGtesting.com
Printed in the USA
FFOW01n1019140616
24912FF

tional foundation under Section 501(c)3 of the Internal Revenue Code.

CATO INSTITUTE

1000 Massachusetts Ave., N.W.

Washington, D.C. 20001

www.cato.org

CPSIA information can be obtained
at www.ICGtesting.com
Printed in the USA
FFOW01n1019140616
24912FF